The Library of SPIDERS

The Tarantula

Alice B. McGinty

Rosen Publishing Group's
PowerKids Press™
New York

To Jake

Published in 2002 by The Rosen Publishing Group, Inc.
29 East 21st Street, New York, NY 10010

First Edition

Book Design: Emily Muschinske
Project Editor: Emily Raabe
Project Consultant: Kathleen Reid Zeiders

Photo Credits: p. 5 (top) © Roger Regeot/David Liebman; p. 5 (bottom) © James Gerholdt/Peter Arnold; p. 6 (top), 13 (top right) © Austin Stevens/Animals Animals; p. 6 (leg), p. 17 (right) © Animals Animals; p. 6 (bottom) © Peter Arnold; p. 7 © Paul Freed/Animals Animals; p. 9, 18 (top), 21 © David Liebman; p. 9 (oval) © Joe Mc Donald/Animals Animals; p. 10 (top) © Ramond A. Mendez/Animals Animals; p. 10 (bottom) © Allan Morgan/Peter Arnold; p. 11, 18 (right) © P. Franklin/Animals Animals; p. 13 (bottom) © John Cooke/Animals Animals; p. 13 (left) © Nigel J. H. Smith/Animals Animals; p. 14 © Microscopix; p.15, 22 © Hans Pfletschiger/Peter Arnold; p. 17 (left) © Doug Wechsler/ Animals Animals.

McGinty, Alice B.
    Tarantula / Alice B. McGinty.— 1st ed.
        p. cm. — (The library of spiders)
    ISBN 0-8239-5566-4 (lib. bdg.)
   1. Tarantulas—Juvenile literature. [1. Tarantulas. 2. Spiders.] I. Title.
    QL458.42.T5 M44 2002
    595.4'4—dc21

                                    00-011697

Manufactured in the United States of America

Contents

The Tarantula

The story of the tarantula began long ago in Taranto, Italy.

In the 1300s, there was a law in Taranto forbidding dancing. Some **peasants** claimed they'd been bitten by a hairy spider. They named it a tarantula. The peasants did a wild dance called the "tarantella" to sweat out the tarantula's deadly **venom**. Of course the government could not forbid dancing that saved lives!

Today scientists don't think Italy's tarantula was deadly. In fact, it was not even the same kind of spider as the American tarantula.

(Left) This tarantula
lives in Mexico.

(Right) This a
red - knee tarantula.

(Below) This is a close-up image of the leg of a curly-haired tarantula.

(Above) Tarantulas often hunt near flowers in order to surprise insects that have come to gather pollen.

Hairy Spiders

The spiders that Americans call tarantulas are part of a family, or group, of spiders named **Hairy Mygalomorphs**. Hairy Mygalomorphs are known by scientists as **primitive** spiders. They have existed for millions of years, yet have changed very little. These spiders open their jaws up and down, and thrust their fangs downward to bite their **prey**. Other spiders, called true spiders, open their jaws from side to side.

There are over 700 **species**, or kinds, of tarantulas in the world. Many live in the wet jungles of South America, Central America, and Africa. Thirty species of tarantulas live in the southwestern United States.

This fully-grown tarantula is only the size of a quarter. Tarantulas can be very small (Right), or as big as an adult's hand (Left).

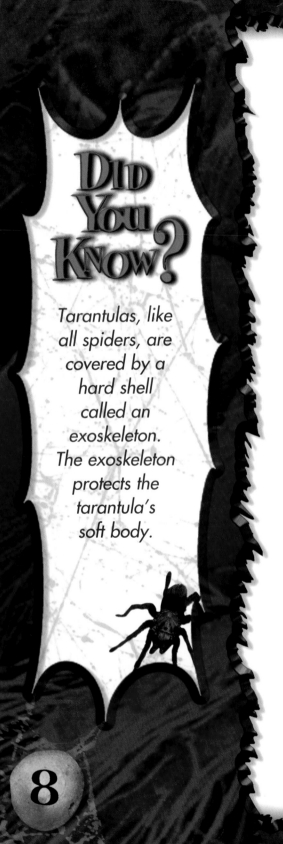

The Tarantula's Body

Tarantulas have two parts to their bodies. The larger body part is the **abdomen**. Inside the tarantula's abdomen are its heart, lungs, and silk glands. Outside are four **spinnerettes**, which release silk.

In front of the abdomen is the spider's other body part. This is called the **cephalothorax**. Attached to the cephalothorax are four pairs of legs and one pair of **pedipalps**. Pedipalps are foot feelers. They look like small legs. The tarantula's jaws, called **chelicerae**, have poison glands inside them. The spider's chelicerae end in sharp fangs.

(Right) This is a close-up of the hair on a tarantula's face.

(Below) This tarantula is clinging to a piece of a cow skull in the desert.

pedipalps

cephalothorax

abdomen

spinnerettes

fangs

(Left) This picture shows the underside of a tarantula. The red area is where the fangs are.

eyes

(Right) This is a tarantula's face. The tiny black dots are the spider's eyes.

How A Tarantula's Body Works

On top of the tarantula's cephalothorax is a hard cap called a **carapace**. The tarantula's eight eyes are on the carapace. Even though they have eight eyes, tarantulas have poor eyesight. Their vision is worse than most spiders. Tarantulas cannot see shapes clearly. They use their eyes to detect light from dark.

The hairs on the tarantula's body sense touch and vibration. Vibrations on the ground and in the air tell the tarantula when another creature is near.

Like all spiders in the Hairy Mygalomorph family, tarantulas have four lungs. Other kinds of spiders have two lungs. Air seeps into a tarantula's lungs through slits in its abdomen.

11

A Tarantula's Home

Tarantulas live in warm parts of the world. Most tarantulas live in underground **burrows**. Many tarantula burrows are underneath stones or dug into hillsides. Tarantulas dig their burrows with their fangs and powerful pedipalps. They line the insides of their burrows with silk. They may even cover the entrance of their burrow with silk.

Many rain forest tarantulas make their homes in trees. Underground burrows might flood, so these tarantulas spin thick, tunnel-shaped webs in the treetops. Special hairs on their feet make them good climbers.

(Above) This red-knee tarantula is looking out of its front door.

Some examples of tarantula homes are, (Below) a nest under a shrub, or (Left) a nest in a tree.

Hunting for Food

Tarantulas come out at night to hunt. They stay close to home as they search for prey. Tarantulas eat insects, especially beetles and grasshoppers. Giant jungle tarantulas also eat frogs, lizards, snakes, and baby birds.

A tarantula knows prey is near when it feels the ground vibrate. It runs toward the vibrations and grabs the prey with its pedipalps. The tarantula raises up on its hind legs, lifts its fangs, and thrusts them down into its prey. The tarantula's venom turns the inside of its prey to liquid. The tarantula sucks out the liquid. It crushes the victim with its strong chelicerae.

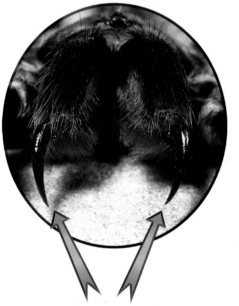

(Right) These are tarantula fangs seen without a microscope.

(Left) This shows what a tarantula's fangs look like under a microscope.

fangs

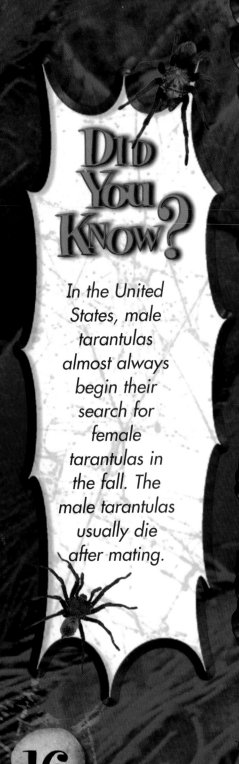

DID YOU KNOW?

In the United States, male tarantulas almost always begin their search for female tarantulas in the fall. The male tarantulas usually die after mating.

Laying Eggs

When male tarantulas are grown, they leave their burrows to search for mates. A chemical in the female tarantula's silk helps the male tarantula find her burrow. The male approaches the female tarantula carefully. She can't see well, and she might confuse him with prey and try to eat him. After mating the male tarantula leaves quickly.

The following summer, the female tarantula spins a cradlelike web in her burrow. She lays 500 to 1,000 eggs in the web. She covers them with silk, and rolls them into a sac. The baby spiders, called spiderlings, will come out in about seven weeks.

(Above) This picture shows the pale belly of a spiderling.

(Right) This tarantula is guarding its eggs, which are hidden in its burrow.

old skin

new skin

(Above) This is a spider molting. The spider's new skin (on the right), is much darker than its old skin. If you look carefully at the old skin, you can see the holes where the spider's fangs used to poke through.

Birth and Growth

When tarantula spiderlings leave their mother's burrow, they must hide. Many of them will be eaten by insects, other spiders, and small animals. The spiderlings dig small homes for themselves nearby.

As the spiderlings grow, their exoskeletons become too small. When this happens, the spiderlings **molt**, or shed their old skin. Their old skin splits, and they crawl out. The spiderlings molt four times a year during their first three years.

Male tarantulas molt until they are fully grown, around 10 to 12 years. Female tarantulas continue to molt after they are grown. Female tarantulas live longer than the males. They can live up to 25 years.

(Left) These young tarantulas are following their mother out of their burrow.

Tarantulas have a patch of barbed hairs on their abdomens. When they rub these hairs with their back legs, the hairs shoot out. These hairs irritate the skin and eyes of predators.

The Tarantula's Enemies

Tarantulas are hunted by weasels, skunks, owls, and snakes. Tarantulas' hairy coats help **camouflage**, or hide, them. If they are discovered, tarantulas rear up and lift their fangs to frighten or to bite predators.

A tarantula's worst enemy is a large wasp called pepsis. This kind of wasp often hunts tarantulas, so it is known as a tarantula hawk. The wasp stings a tarantula, **paralyzing** it. The wasp lays an egg on the helpless tarantula and then buries the spider alive. When the egg hatches, the wasp **larva** eats the tarantula.

(Right) This photo shows the pepsis wasp.

Tarantulas and People

Since tarantulas stay in their burrows during the day, people do not see them often. In the fall, male tarantulas can be found wandering in search of mates. Many of these males are killed on highways.

Big, hairy tarantulas look frightening, but they are really shy, peaceful creatures. Tarantulas usually only bite people if they are treated roughly. Their bites hurt about as much as a bee sting. There are tarantulas that are poisonous. Tarantulas from the United States, however, are not known to be poisonous. Tarantulas can make good pets. They live long lives and have many interesting habits.

Glossary

abdomen (AB-duh-min) A spider's larger, rear body part.

camouflage (KA-muh-flahj) The color or pattern of an animal's fur, feathers, or skin, that allows it to blend in and not be seen.

carapace (CAR-uh-payc) A hard cap on top of the spider's cephalothorax.

cephalothroax (sef-uh-low-THOR-ax) A spider's smaller, front body part, containing its head and chest.

chelicerae (cheh-LIHS-eh-ray) A spider's "jaws" containing the fangs.

family (FAM-ih-lee) The scientific name of a group of plants or animals which are alike in some ways.

Hairy Mygalomorphs (HAR-ee mih-GAL-oh-morfs) A family of spiders, also called Theraphosidae, with primitive features.

larva (LAHR-vuh) The form of a baby insect after it hatches from its egg and before it changes into an insect.

molt (MOHLT) The shedding of the outer layer of skin or hair.

paralyzing (PAR-uh-lyzing) Causing something to be unable to move.

peasants (PEZ-ents) People in Europe who worked on farms or in the country.

pedipalps (PED-ih-palps) Two short "feelers" attached to the cephalothorax.

prey (PRAY) An animal which is hunted and eaten by another animal.

species (SPEE-shees) Groups of animals or plants that are very much alike.

spinnerettes (spin-uhr-ETZ) Organs located on the rear of the spider's abdomen which release silk.

venom (VEN-um) A poison passed by one animal into another through a bite or sting.

Index

Web Sites

To learn more about tarantulas, check out these Web sites:

www.sfzoo.org/map.insectzoo.html
www.tarantulas.com/main.htm